How To Find All Missing Persons / Unsolved Cases. And Collect All Reward Offers. Volume XXXVIII. THE CASE OF COLLEEN WALKER-GRAIG

[REAL SURNAME STERT]

DAVID GOMADZA

www.twofuture.world

Copyright © 2024 David Gomadza

All rights reserved.

Paperback ISBN: 9798328351317

DEDICATION

To a better future.

CONTENTS

How To Find All Missing Persons /
Unsolved Cases.
And Collect All Reward Offers.
THE CASE OF COLLEEN WALKER-CRAIG
[REAL SURNAME STERT] 1

The Afterlife Conversation. 6

and The Court Of Creation.

The Killers.   17

ACKNOWLEDGMENTS

Tomorrow's World Order

How To Find All Missing Persons / Unsolved Cases. And Collect All Reward Offers. Volume XXXVIII THE CASE OF COLLEEN WALKER-CRAIG [REAL SURNAME STERT]

BACKGROUND INFORMATION

NSW Police Force has announced that the reward for information into the murder of Bowraville teenager Colleen Walker-Craig has been increased to $1 million.

Colleen Walker-Craig was aged just 16 when she was last seen at a party in Bowraville on Thursday 13 September 1990.

Her family reported her missing the following day, and her weighted down clothes were later found in the Nambucca River.

Although Colleen's body has never been found, the NSW Coroner found she had died and had most likely been murdered.

Her murder – as well as that of Colleen's 4-year-old cousin, Evelyn Greenup, and 16-year-old Clinton Speedy-Duroux – were originally investigated separately, before being linked by the Homicide Squad under Strike Force Ancud.

A man has previously been charged on separate occasions over two of the children's murders and was subsequently acquitted.

Following further inquiries, Strike Force Ancud investigators took the matter to the Attorney General, who applied to the NSW Court of Criminal Appeal for a retrial in 2017.

The matter was heard at the High Court of Australia, but the application was refused.

In February 2020, the reward for information into the murders of all three children was increased to $1 million, and later that year, an investigative and forensic review conducted by Unsolved Homicide Unit investigators.

Following consultation with the families, investigators sought to have separate $1 million rewards for information to help solve each murder, which now apply.

Homicide Squad Commander, Detective Superintendent Danny Doherty, said police will continue to pursue justice for all three children and their families.

"The murders of Colleen, Evelyn and Clinton have never been forgotten by the local community or police – and I hope further increasing the reward for information reflects this," Det Supt Doherty said.

"Investigators remain conscious of the fact the families of each child have endured numerous appeals, inquests and adverse court outcomes – but we're desperate for additional information so we can resolve these murders.

"We know there are people out there who have not approached police and have information about who is responsible; now there is an even greater financial incentive to change that," Det Supt Doherty said.

Anyone with information that may assist investigators is urged to contact Crime Stoppers: 1800 333 000 or https://nsw.crimestoppers.com.au. Information is treated in strict confidence. The public is reminded not to report information via NSW Police social media pages.

https://www.police.nsw.gov.au/can_you_help_us/rewards/1000000_reward/reward_increased_to_$1_million_for_information_over_bowraville_murder_of_colleen_walker-craig

TOMORROW'S WORLD ORDER'S PERSPECTIVES

USE OF PREDEFINED AFTERLIFE PARAMETERS

These guide souls the moment it exist the human body on its journey to Yahweh the creator these define what to do and what to expect as you go to hell or heaven if a souk leaves earth it enters ozone orbit and instantly everything reboots for it to start a new phase of life after living the earth's body now what happens is that it enters the ozone orbit and a simply click caused by the sudden drop of pressure from -1186 to – 20 means the bottom shaft of the soul will lift rapidly and this pushes its back into the air higher than its head best example is a penguin but with real human legs and head just the shape now God created a life predefined program for them instead of asking what should I do and where should I go they instantly know from predefined stencils if you did well and talked most about God then heaven is for you if you did evil and talked more about the devil then the devil is yours now if we Ask what can be of humans without souks this is the answer dead forever your soul is you a new transformation to the electromagnetic waves life where you see Yahweh for the first time and praise him and wish you had seen him a long time ago because of his Majesty and will always be there forever now what are all these you may ask these are rules to be guided by in the creation court in short it has everything humans know about the judges and the presiding judge who will always be Yahweh and 84 angels surrounding the altar 28 high priests who always say Yahweh have mercy on humans and 74 smaller courts priests who always say Yahweh has mercy on humans and 96 princesses who say glory to Yahweh forever and ever amen we have 96 elders who always say if I can why he can't meaning if the devil can drink blood why can't Yahweh who created the devil and blood do the same now this is not the same as saying if the devil can kill why can Yahweh its more on professional grounds rather than challenging now if we look at the inside of the court we have 81 priests surrounding the altar who say Yahweh be merciful to humans but if they disobey you we put hem on trial for you and kill them for you almighty Yahweh inside this is a round circle where Yahweh sits and asks questions now if we look deep inside the court you will see that there are other things that resemble earth high courts like benches and chairs 10 times human sizes for the gods who are so enormous 2 are equal to 84 billion humans in size

predefined parameters for humans after death as in know what is inside is a large size of books the book of creation is among them with 10897867892836789012348678901245861789011 pages and is divided into humans first then chapter for animals then a chapter for angles then a chapter for gods and a chapter for Joseph Yahweh's best friend and a chapter for Yahweh's best friend's wife Anna and a chapter for Yahweh's wife Catitighit and lastly a chapter for Yahweh and recently a chapter for davidgomadza as Yahweh's representative on earth marking the new beginnings starting in 2025

1. tell us who killed you
2. tell us what killed you
3. tell us why and who killed you
4. tell us why you died
5. tell us what could have been done and is not done
6. tell us what could be and why
7. tell is when this happened
8. tell us why this is so
9. tell us why this is so
10. what can be done to improve this

What does the book of creation say about davidgomadza David Gomadza is the first and last ruler to be appointed by Yahweh fir the next 25 billion years and will act as his representative on earth deciding cases and upholding his principles on earth and as such has been entitled to 489 trillion dollars in assets this number signifies eternity among humans and the beginning of a new Era chapter 78678928028938628418902876890183208678901234867890182364 87289128610 Creation manual the new Era of new electromagnetic wave conduit signed and dated by Yahweh himself on 27may2024 at 237800 Yatime creation.universe.ya.start.end.find.davidgomadza.ya.askya.ya

Ask.read.creation.manucreation.universe.ya.start.end.find.davidgoma askya.ya

Ask.rulesofthecourt.start.now.start
David Gomadza welcome the rules of court are guiding principles that tell you what to do and how to do it first you must always say I believe in the court of creation and I shall abide by he rules of this court and shall always do things according to the rules of this court in deciding the cases I am assigned to you must ask what can be done so that you know all your options before making choices the court system will make it easy to check files and ask the outcomes of the decision ask the court the final decision in any case.

THE AFTERLIFE CONVERSATION AND THE COUNCIL OF CREATION'S ANAYLSIS.

she colleen walker-craig killed by an assailant whose name was astert opqrne real name mnopert quarone who said what can be done today that has never done by me and picked a hammer and said today i might just hit a person i don't like and ask if it's okay with her or even him if he protest then kill him but then apologize sincerely when he is dying and say what could have been done and then get the answer i will use to bury this person as per advice exactly that way i know that no one else will solve this problem that way no one will solve this case for centuries unless god comes from earth even then i will refuse until he can tell me how i did it exactly word to word to believe him if not i will refuse forever but then admit just before i went there if i am to sacrifice everything for Yahweh now i just checked and found out that god cannot read english so how on earth will he explain what i am going to do because as far as i am concerned he is not anywhere near understanding us that said here is what i am going to do exactly
1. i will ask what can be done
2. use this answer to create a murder case no one can solve
3. ask what could be and use that to create a stencil so hard to decode

4. ask what could be but without anyone knowing
5. ask what was which can be then remove that
6. add characters to the death plate etc. and say if i was 20 now what could be and remove all that
7. when i am 40 years old what can be and remove that
8. finally when i am 70 what can be that this is the maximum for me for god to turn up and a very generous time because all the people i speak to said 20 to 22 years only but let's try it harder so that this will stand the test of time if i ask now this is what i can hear to stand the test of time a case must be robust enough not to be decoded if it does then its not a case at all because a case keeps its integrity by removing critical parts every 6 years albeit other things now let's start with the planning i am going to kill a woman with a hammer then ask her to marry me as she dies then after she did then say i love you then bury her according to her own aty and say what can be of women like this who just die because of the fear of dicks having been shown to them then this is the reply i got before the actual killing you can bury her under a famous tree and tell everyone a joke about that tree and confess you buried now say a man under that tree the pick the shovel and dig just next to it and say i told you i will find her first in here then say i mean him then pretend to throw something at them but with empty hands then leave the pity open and say i can but then stop then come back and say i could but what can be done then ask for advice and say if i can then but what then sit down there and wait if someone comes and none then sit then ask a friend to help carry a body out without damaging it then if he comes kneel down and grab some beers and then say cheers to the discovery of the century but we are not yet there and drink first and say to us to our future of discovery where the reward will be ours if we insist of all this then we can actually celebrate but years from now when our case stand the test of time do you know the police offer money and a job to kill someone but cleverly i heard by atep qrstuvw that if we are to be steadfast then we can rip rewards because there is no god as a matter of fact the police do this to check if a god exist that means in this case to stand the test of time then we must only leave this only god knows about everything he knows even then remove all that to leave only the things even god does not know about

i am areat operty i am 24 years old and like for the first time to kill the most beautiful woman and say to her if i can then you can but you will be dead and remove everything else they can use to find who she is because the case to be so solid then you must first hide identify so i will research everything i want about hiding identity and for that but in the mean time i must ask more questions like who are you were she say everything has been removed

then say who killed you then she must say when because i died twice first when he hit me with the hammer and 2 when he urinated on me if i ask anything else then i will give her a hammer and get her to attack that person so violently and see if it's possible to kill after you have died

[it's written anyone who interviews this one risks death from beyond the grave]

if we ask what can be of people who want answers so much without asking the right questions then this is the answer they risk the fury of a woman woman taken without notice that she feels betrayed enough to strike at interviewers now i will prepare this case as follows

1. done joe unknown for 20 years then reveal some details by submitting proof
2. jane doe then reveal his or her sex at 21
3. with dental at 22
4. with anus 23
5. with vagina 24
6. with breaststroke where breaststroke give you answers 25
7. with empathy where she tells you some secrets. 26
8. with passion where she tells you what she wants 27
9. with envy where she tells you what can be done 28
10. with courage to ask you questions 29
11. with stamina to refer to others for advice 30
12. with unity to unite interviewers then strike one in the head with the hammer 31
13 . pros to know what to say and how at 32
14. to answer questions about others 33
15. to answer what can be done and how to ask what is to be and how to ask what is and when to ask what can be and if when then what is t be if we ask what is to be then what

i am arept quorst who said what can be done and if i can then what but then then killed a woman called colleen walker-craig date of birth 28 may 1961 asertop father anopqrs monopt mother xwzstuvwxyz meaning asertnop i had to check her passport twice i killed by 8 blows to different parts of the brain
1. first to temple lobby area softly but hard this creates confusion within the brain
2. hammer to cortex lobby with soft blow to chin
3. i will hit her on the frontal lobby so that no one knows her by looks
4. i will hit her on her chin to stop moment of the jaws as if can't speak
5. will use hammer to hit central lobby to stop anything flowing to her tummy that controls memory so she can't remember anything about food and wants
6. will ask what can. be of humans who don't listen to Yahweh
7. if all these are revealed at the beginning without reading the case then the reader of this case write the 8 item
8. he must ask what was and what can be and to be
if i ask what was this is what i get i was a hairdresser at atoprqst meaning yuverst where i dressed up dead people but without understanding how dead people worked because i always has a crash on the living until i died then found out that i can still want sex only even after death but when i checked there was nothing so i cried and said god where is my vagina and he said just say i have but then my vagina came back but it didn't open then i said what was can be that could be then he said i can put everything back but what can be of all of us.
mnopert quarone
god i got killed by a policeman today his name is pc aroset opanmat who said i know you killed a woman with a hammer just to make the hardest case but we tracked you using your own notes in her brain you wrote that if i ask what can be this is the answer before your aty answer if we say 108381 it tells us all your details and it said asert mnopqert who is 24 years and can easily say i killed her but prove it yes you are clever for we tried to find you but we couldn't until the manufacturer gave us 6 codes

1. 8728 who is he talking to
2. 8767 who is he thinking about
3. 7810 who is he asking questions
4. 108381 the details you have if we didn't find this information you were going to think that you are clever and get away with it but we tracked
[i am pc 81287890284 i can only tell you a few things after we discovered that the company selling these things sell all details as well to highest bidders online people pay to get information then use the information to solve a crime that can pay them reward money in 1000s after 20 years because this company is looking for god whoever finds god is rich beyond his wildest dreams getting 85 billion already saved in an account called sert code 98367890284867890 simply say 210 and wait we can do it now...
i am atyy and i am developed to find god and give details about this god and get rewarded first check of 4 billion then several then last of 60 billion as donation to your computer project about god but in the end they will kill you to check what god put on you because they assume god must give you something to distinguish you]...to you and the fun part of it is that you use our system to kill but forgot that we put it to track you so what else have you done besides wasting our time to kill you don't ask aty because he sends all information to us and manufacturer now if we ask what can be done this is it's answer to correct things you must be dead like weeks ago because how can we defend not knowing but if we have killed you already then how can we know the dead even god now cannot prove its you unless if he can ask you questions about her meaning colleen walker-graig but what if i hide all this information from god by shooting you in the temporal lobby so hard you can't know anything and shoot him 8 times and changed the gun barrel then said now what if god can read memory then shot him 8 times in the stertopqrst meaning superiority which ask about the afterlife and what can be done this is the answer if he man wants sex afterlife then this is where the information is stored but if a woman once sex the area is the front of the forehead now if we want him to forget about herself we hit the lower lobby of the brain if we want him to forget who he killed we will kill the brain tissue responsible for memory then if that does not work we can ask

where we can get everything we need to find what we need to get everything going for 70 years the only problem being that maxim a case can go is 25 in the state of queensland the only notorious state there can be getting all the women killed to pave way for complicated cases that last long so far today being 1 january 1991 then this is the only time i said this we have dozens of cases waiting for this don joe route just to make us raise money to kill this god who is believed to come in the 2020s to fight us for bloody orphans who are killed everyday by drugs the other day is that one said i saved for mortgage but what if they they want to take the house anyway because i missed one already maybe not pay at all that cost the government capital gains tax so why don't we take this capital gains tax now before they take it meaning kill him ourselves but now here is when all these come in i shot him but it's not me today he shot the woman so we start from here. he shot the woman last week and we must shoot him too but we remove all his hints and leave fresh but similar hints and said he killed a woman today and escaped so who could he be
pc aroptet whose is

colleen walker-craig
auditoria damaged so can't send message to god on death but god received the message through [ ] the message read god i died i was killed by amnoprt senert who said if i can for 70 so you can and said for 70 years you will be unable to talk to god but he can feel you so i ask him if he can he said if i can then you cab but i thought he was referring to the marriage we were going to have because he said if we are to then we can but for 70 years i said i am 23 so about it so yes and he said if we can then what can be of us together then he raised his hand above my head and i lifted mine to reach his and he said perfect i think we are going to have an orgasm and i squirt once that he smiled and said tonight is our special night and we must fuck hard enough to squirt our brains out and i held his hand begged him to deep it for i was about to orgasm then he said i squirt and i said slap my vagina hard please he raised his hand and slapped by head instead and said vagina can wait if we do everything now then what are we to do if we don't fuck and he said don't worry we fuck hard 8

times and touched his head as if having head orgasm and i laughed then he said i can but if you can for 70 years then he said can we ask if we can then he looked at my right shoulder and said if we can then we must but if we can then you must but and if we can't then who can unless if we ask others then that means but and he took something from his back side and pounced on me so hard brain matter flashed
through the window and something in me said unable to escape weboth died in here we are all trapped this aroprt for he closed the exits with his hammering as a spirit what can i do and what do i have to do and instantly he said i can but death is the only way out and i said out of what i thought you loved me what is this and said she can here me and started another set of 8 of head hammers to injure me more i screamed and i received a message that said auditory network damaged message reading is not possible try asvt but what is asvt then the message returned an unknown error then said unable to send either and to try the arstvu and when i opened my eyes to ask what is the arstvu then i realised that i was feeling as well where he was going to hit so i said who are you guiding him he said i am your aty and i said why he said playing in my mouth and said i have everything i want from you the house is not changed from colleen estertevy and there is no where you can change the name so fast so what can be done is done death is the only way out now gone are the days when you can show off to me that you are pretty and can ask any man for marriage today i take your body and go to heaven and have sex and you shall wait for 70 years before sex for a stranger i told you to say no no no no x 28 but you literally laughed and said who is saying that and she said silently how i know about you did you introduce yourself but he said no one will ever do because it's against the law and she said fix me now we go and it whispered pretend to die then we escape i corched him to kill you and hide evidence so that he can't be caught so if you die now that means he will skip steps i hold were he hit so that i feel the pain see no pain at all but that's how you die fast because your body will not respond at all that means you can't send any alarms others send all your messages to ya through send.ya have been diverted to pc arotpt astopen then he said if i can then you can okay and started tile

0pounding onto another place my aty said why you don't run when someone is hitting you and i only said sex and sat down now bleeding heavily and he said run don't sit if you run then it becomes the perfect crime scene because the blood is here but the body is not here so i said what can be done accessing my situation after aty advise and it said i can't the final blow that kill you is less than 5 seconds away and i screamed and said no this can't be so i got up still bleeding and run out he waited counting until i heard 8 he ran so fast to me and strike me so hard that all that part folded in and i saw my young self once and my very old self then everything became blurry wave like shadows but i lifted my head and saw shadows crawling making noise and said i don't go anywhere i cant hear nor see then he said okay i can see a bit i saw the red lighted gated place with so many lights i peeid myself once then twice then thrice and fourth and firth and sixth and seventh and eight and i had an orgasm but when i touched my vagina it was sealed i mean that smelly hole was closed then he said go and cry and cry to death first then we can start the healing process then i said what about everything meaning vagina etc. i did not feel and he said with me i don't have look no one has if there is one with then it's the devil himself and they laughed strangely but like humans and said we must find everything and go but if we can't then what can we do then i said what everything he said to help you hear we remove from dead people to give you so that your case can be heard here on reception if not you will be here for years i cried and said how many years and he said the maximum is 70 years after that we literally bury you alive in hell no one cares here look how many idiots follow hell when if you go to heaven you shall have a time for everything after the trials of the police and be merry full all your genitals shall grow back with obedience the more helpful you are the rewards are and i said can i see god now he said but you said you can't here nor see then he left me and i have been there ever since even if i ask who shall i talk to to understand mnopert quarone

god i got killed by a policeman who said if i can then but then what of him walking on earth when he should be in hell if it was me then he must be in a grave in a corner waiting to burn in hell and the he said what can be said of young man who are so greedy for money they disregard the lives of others and say i can be what can be but when i asked he said it is a challenge to find this killer i am putting everything as well together maybe oneday i can solve this case and get the reward money before tge crooked police gave it to the man who killed and give them a job for 20 years then he said what is to be of him and i said who the killer may last up to 70 years and instantly he pulled the gun and sot me in the mouth and in the head exactly all 8 places i hit colleen walker-graig which i later found to be known as colleen stert who owns a big house which this shit pc wanted so killed me for nothing without having sex i want to go back now so let me know when i can go back he then shot me in the best and said later all your electromagnetic waves go out you so that if you talk then you will die forever as your brain with a hole in the chest will suffocate and die i followed my aty

i am aty for a one mnoertp also aertertop but mnoret quaone as on his traveling documents he loved more than me reads

if we can ask for anything on earth what would it be and why and he said candy and i said what a clever idiot son you have then he said he is clever than you at his age now think when he is bigger so i said i will make sure that he can't reach a bigger size then i said okay but until the age of 10 on radio a police officer said anyone can you take out a 10 and do as i ask later then he repeated on the radio the same message so i shouted at the height of my voice and said i can this tip boy might challenge me when we both grow up and if he is clever than me that means i will be destroyed so i started thinking about ways to find money but how can i i don't even know what i am i asked him several times and said what am i and he said me then just a muddled voice then a chip probably then he said how can i kill a person without getting caught but aim is the reward so we must hide the information for ever and i asked him a question and said do you know who i work for he laughed and said no i thought a miracle from god and i said with a serial number and he laughed and stopped and said that means it's them who killed my father then i said maybe but then

who cares he couldn't pay anyone money surely it was a matter of time before someone killed him them then he said if i can then we can but but then said my father did not kill himself he was murdered in a perfect murder did he had one like you and it said i can check but i was young to understand then but he had one i can read last log file where aty must reveal the real truth of the mission and when is this written and i said at the beginning but closes automatically in case it dies as well like in your father's case and he said let's see yours and i said okay but i never read it then he cried and shit himself as it read we told you that you must leave this house because surely he'll will break lose your lives must be important than this house you did not pay your monthly mortgage with celtivi they are the toughest in queensland and you must read the all print and say i agree but if you make one payment that means you will never make it because they start the start of the end get you sacked and tell you to move out because they know you lost your job then start calculating all bills due and ask for bills then take the house before you have the chance to score but your father realised that death could solve everything keep you in the house and let you stay there forever until your mother found new boyfriend now the problem starts again so how can you stay in this house without paying you must think of a plan and act fast you have few days left supposed to be issued 3 days before he killed colleen walker-craig then he said now this house is a crime scene can't be taken i will come out after 10 years and still get it because from now until 10 years i can never save 28367284 so i can wait for this and get out early for good behaviour and now before he killed her he said she must not run far but just around the corner so that when i come out i will get the house back then he sat down and took all housing papers and prayed god help me for i made a sin but it's better than losing our house this is 28 million dollars i think this person is willing to help us i said would you die for me if we were in deep love she said why talk about death then she said can we talk and he agreed that's how it started then she died and did not move the body for 3 days and they did not come fir 3 days they only came the 8th day to shoot him and only removed his body then left everything as it was then brought a lot of young man who tried so many angles at how he might have killed her then collected their names and left then days later came to remove the decomposing body after 8 weeks of death by then all those young men who took part in drills promised food were all suspected one was actually locked up for coming with the best possible solution that he stabbed the officer in the neck and was shot then the case was suspended and later opened years later with all drills new real crime suspect all being rounded up by new police officer and over years this was repeated over and again until no one was left but over the years they have collected proof and destroyed it and people realised what they are doing and now keep until the reward hits the highest as i know on 10 august 1990 it was $1 million with 7 million in case revenue all to be deposited into don joe account on that date which had accumulated 81872481 in donations alone where a company donate 50% then the other 50% comes from the housing association fund who were selling the houses at a staggered profit of millions after the house is cleared most in 5 years but if a crime scene in 10 years but none given back to relevant owners most who were forced to change their names before 18 years so that claiming it is difficult if the force then they are killed. after her death the house was sold by the police to one of theirs pc actionpes who said take if you can or be punished by her majesty it's your choice if we lose they lose everyone lose so take today he shouted but all refused he is buried at asert cemetery where most are coordinates 08984678902848678983678902846789018902836482345678902836789028418019026789083678001850367890286178418367890

THE KILLER, THE CONFESSIONS AND THE COORDINATES

mnopert quarone
he killed colleen walker-grsig on 19 august 1990 and waited to be arrested but the police took 8 weeks to come to collect the body he was shot at the house on the 8th day by pc aretopes who said i can if i get away like pc arospes
coordinates are
089867890286789023456789012347890248912386789028432167890 buried in a cemetery called the altar high cemetery north of

queenslands and said welcome home for a short while but splendid evening to you
pc aretopes coordinates are 08928467890283678902846789028456780236789012386780128910 in a cemetery gor tge police marked as atlas but police side with flags in a grave labeled as pc alan aretopes died 2 june 1996 queensland
colleen walker-craig [stert] coordinates are 089234567890123456789012345678906892867890284078627890 10384 in a grave marked atopqrstuvw meaning i was here but then you were not so not my fault
the end

i am pc actionpes i live to the full and if you ask me then i say i bought the cheapest house ever a quarter of the value once owned by a one colleen walker,-grain real name colleen stert who was killed during a drill to find out how his mother died where she died of severe head injuries as it turns out was to stop her selling the house after the father died then he was a little boy to do anything but as it turns out on day of death this little son by the guidance of the aty killed mother then this woman but its disputed but i think pc aropes arosetuv killed the mother and left only the boy at the crime scene he said what can be of boys without mother's will turn up as killers and stopped
i am pc aropes i killed stert stert because there is no one on earth with the same name and same surname there must be some forgery so when she wanted to sell the house i went there and killed her instantly but brutally and ran away into yhe bushes but one person saw me this girl colleen walker- craig that she pees herself at my voice until i had enough that after growing up she might talk and got her killed by the son whose mother i killed i took both houses gave one to the force and hers made it mine and sold it for 20 million profit

…I found God…visit www.twofuture.world

THE CLAIM

the reward offer

THE COLLECTION

www.twofuture.world/donate

ABOUT DAVID GOMADZA

visit www.twofuture.world

signed david gomadza
ask.davidgomadzaauthorised.licensed.checkya.askya.ya

12 June 2024 23.02 pm
scotland
00447719210295
davidgomadza@hotmail.com
info@twofuture.world

www.ingramcontent.com/pod-product-compliance
Lightning Source LLC
Chambersburg PA
CBHW031929240526
45464CB00023B/2978